KU-453-103

For Mum & Dad

Text copyright © Andrew Donkin 1996
Illustrations copyright © Amanda Harvey 1996

First published in 1996

First published in Great Britain in 1996
by Macdonald Young Books
61 Western Road
Hove
East Sussex BN3 1JD

Designed and Typeset by Backup... Design and Production, London
Printed and bound in Belgium by Proost International Book Production

British Library Cataloguing in Publication Data available

ISBN 0 7500 2175 6
ISBN 0 7500 2176 4 (pb)

ANDREW DONKIN

Night Skies

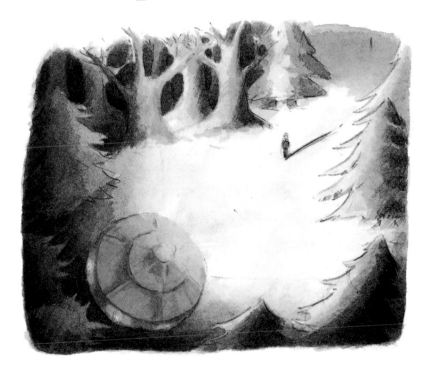

Illustrated by Amanda Harvey

MACDONALD YOUNG BOOKS

Chapter One

At last. We finally arrive. We have driven all the way up to Scotland to sort out my great uncle's house. Mum's old uncle. We're staying in the house for a day or two. It's empty now.

I only saw him once when I was very small and I don't remember what he looked like.

He used to write letters to me though. I've kept all of them. I have one in my pocket right now.

We arrive at the house at 5 o'clock on a winter's afternoon. We are in the middle of the Scottish countryside. The middle of nowhere. I get out of the car and stretch my legs. The air smells cold and clean.

The house is larger than I expected. It has thin rattly windows that would get broken into if you lived where we did. The large grounds slope away into woodlands.

The sun falls behind the trees and a great dark shadow stretches across where we are standing on the grass.

"Come on, it's freezing," says Mum, as she begins fumbling in her handbag. She is looking for the house keys that the solicitor sent.

I reach inside my coat and touch the letter. It was the last letter he wrote before he died. In it, he told me about something hidden in the house. A secret. When I first read it, I thought it was just a story he was making up to amuse me.

Mum finds the house keys. We are nine hours and four hundred miles from home. Standing in the twilight chill, suddenly I'm not so sure that he was making it up.

I touch the letter in my pocket again and shudder. Mum opens the front door.

"Don't you want to get inside?" she asks.

I smile uneasily.

Chapter Two

The house is full of old fashioned furniture. The whole place smells damp and musty. There's dust everywhere.

We dump our bags upstairs. The house is as cold as an icebox. Mum goes down to light the old stove in the kitchen. I open up the bedroom window and look out over the grounds.

Everything is silent. I peer up at the darkening sky and think about his letter.

Suddenly, I hear the sound of beefburgers sizzling in the kitchen. Ten minutes later, Mum calls.

"Food's ready!"

Neither of us really enjoys supper. Somehow the burgers taste stale like the house.

Next day we drive into the local village.
Uncle was very old and didn't go out
much. Hardly anyone got to know him.

Mum talks to the grocer. He says he'll
prepare the bill for the last month's food
deliveries. Mum hadn't seen her uncle for
years so doesn't get upset. As we get into
the car again, it starts to rain.

Back at the house, I go upstairs and take out the letter.

It was written during the last days of his illness. The handwriting is scrawly and hard to understand. The black ink smudges on my fingers, but I read it again anyway.

In the 1950s, my great uncle was a spy for the government. When she was little, Mum used to get stamps and postcards from him from all over the world.

In 1954, he was in Vovnaya, a town in the snowy bit of Russia. He mixed with the local people and heard rumours from the foothills outside the town.

This time the rumour was that a UFO had fallen from the sky and crashed.

My great uncle and another spy went out to the foothills. The letter says that they found a space ship only 5 metres long.

Inside were a crew of small creatures wearing bright shiny uniforms.

His letter says that they told no one
of their find, but he brought one of the
creatures home. He says that it is in the
wine store. No one else knows. Not Mum.
No one.

I stop reading and look over my
shoulder. I shudder, thinking of the
skeleton that may be sharing the house
with us.

Chapter Three

Mum starts sorting out some of uncle's stuff. I get my torch and open the cellar door. It creaks like mad, but Mum is too far away to hear.

I get to the bottom of the stairs and shine the torch into the darkness. The cellar is huge. I begin to look round.

There are packing cases stuffed with books and papers and other junk. I search carefully. The closest I come to a wine store is a few empty bottles lying on the floor. It's not here. The whole thing is just a story. I feel relieved.

Then something touches my shoulder. I spin round and it drops on my face.

It's sticky.

"Ugh!"

I've walked into a spider's web.

I brush it away, but it's all in my hair and everywhere. A bit goes in my mouth.

I go upstairs and wipe it off just before Mum sees me.

For the first time since we arrived, I feel relaxed. I snuggle under the warm bedclothes as Mum tucks me in.

"You seem to have brightened up," she says. I ask Mum about the lack of wine in the cellar.

"Oh no," she says, "the wine store is not in the cellar. It's in one of the outhouses."

My stomach flips like it's on a roller coaster.

As soon as Mum goes to sleep I put on my dressing-gown and creep downstairs and out of the house.

Midnight. The sky is clear and full of stars.

I don't have to look far to find the right outhouse. Inside are rows and rows of bottles. I'm quite hot by now. I guess I'm worried the skeleton may be here after all.

I move quickly through the maze of wine racks. At the back, I see something and stop dead. There's a freezer. A large freezer.

I open the door. Inside is a crate with strange writing on the side. I spot the word "Russia". Inside the crate is a large block of ice. As I lean forward, cold air flows out of the freezer and over my face. I look inside.

Chapter Four

I am staring into the block of ice. Inside is a body. A small body about one metre long.

It could be a monkey or a small person or anything. The ice is frosty and however hard I look, I cannot make out what it is.

I bend forwards and my hand touches the ice. I jerk it back, but the ice is so cold that my fingers stick to it for a second.

I don't know what to do. I look round. The freezer hums quietly to itself. By the side is a large control switch. The last setting is "defrost". I reach out for the switch.

It won't move. Stuck. Rusted after years of just sitting there. I take a good grip and try really hard. The metal switch digs into my fingers, but it still won't budge. I use the sleeve of my dressing-gown to get a better grip and twist it. My heart is really beating hard now.

I nearly snap my fingers off when suddenly the control moves. I almost fall on to the ice. It's done.

The freezer hums louder as it clicks into defrost mode. I stand back. By morning the ice will be melted and I will see what is really inside.

I leave and hurry back towards the house. The ground is silver in the moonlight. The stars are sharp diamonds in a dark sky. They look much brighter and closer than they do in the city.

I get into bed. It takes me forever to go to sleep.

Chapter Five

Morning. When I wake up it's much later than I expect. I get dressed and think about the night before.

"You look tired," says Mum, fussing. I try not to yawn. Mum has done horrible fried mushrooms for breakfast. When she's not looking, I sneak them into a tissue and get rid of them.

I get out at last and walk towards the outhouse. In my head I replay the memory of looking into the ice. Soon I will know. I thought it would be less scary in the daytime, but it isn't. I open the door. Inside, shadows lurk menacingly at every corner.

I hear the sound of dripping water. I walk towards it. Slowly. I turn the corner and look. The floor around the refrigerator is covered with a pool of water.

I realize something is missing. It's not there. The thing in the ice is gone.

I start looking around in case someone has moved it or something. The dripping of the water kind of spooks me and I get a bit hot and panicked.

"Hey!"

Someone shouts at me and I jump about a million miles. It's Mum calling from the house.

"Where are you? Get over here!"

Disaster. Mum makes me go with her into the nearest town. She has to see the solicitor. I sit outside his office for hours. His secretary keeps telling me that Mum won't be long. She is.

Worse is to come. We go shopping. "We" buy a tartan golf towel which I am to give to Dad on my next visit.

By the time we drive back to great uncle's house, it is twilight. Mum does not want to travel all the way home on the motorway in the dark. We have to stay here for one more night.

I know that whatever was in the ice couldn't still be alive. But I'm a bit worried anyway.

As we walk to the house I see that the first stars are appearing in the sky. We go inside. I lock the door behind us. Just in case.

Chapter Six

I watch night fall. There are no street lights or other houses anywhere around. The old farmhouse is surrounded by nothing but darkness.

I sit in the kitchen as Mum begins to make supper.

"I bought some of your favourites in town," she says grinning. I decide not to tell her anything. What could I say?

I sit there, thinking about getting my torch and searching the house. Then I hear it.

There is something scratching the back door. It sounds like a claw scraping against the wood. It is low down near the floor.

Something is trying to get in. Mum hears it too.

Then there is a proper knock on the
door, Mum moves towards it.

"Mum don't," I blurt out, but it is too
late. She opens the door.

Outside is the grocer from the village.
At his feet is a black collie dog. Mum pays
the outstanding bill and gives me a strange
look.

After we have eaten, Mum goes upstairs for a bath. She leaves me reading a book, but I can't really concentrate. I suppose I am a little jumpy by now.

I am listening hard for any more sounds. That's when I hear it. It is like a distant vibration. Then I realize it is an engine. It is getting nearer, approaching the front of the house. I stand up.

Suddenly a bright white light blasts through the window. It is blinding and fills the whole room. I cover my eyes.

The light swerves away and I hear voices.

I run to the front door. Outside is a small green jeep. Inside it are four teenagers, two girls and two boys, from the local village.

"Did you see them?" asks the driver in a Scottish accent.

"See what?"

"Lights in the sky. Weird coloured lights. We've been chasing them."

Before I can speak, one of them points to the horizon and they speed off.

I don't think twice. I close the door behind me and walk out into the dark. I have to know.

Chapter Seven

Outside it's colder than last night. I'm running and my breath makes clouds of mist in front of me.

I see the jeep with the teenagers disappear behind a line of trees. I head in their direction for a while, but then something makes me go into the woods. Everything is silent. The trees glisten with frost. The sky is clear. I gaze up at the stars.

I walk through the woods looking
around in every direction. I keep
watching, but there is nothing to see. Just
stars, frozen still in the night.

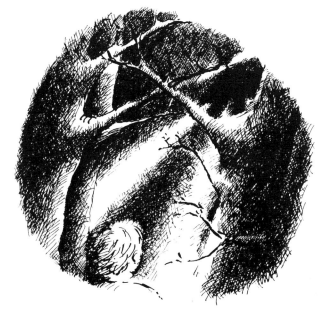

Then ahead in the trees, I spot a light.
My heart jumps until I realize that it must
be the teenagers. They have gone into the
woods as well.

I decide to head towards them. I want
to ask them what they saw. If they really
saw anything.

As I get nearer their torches go red then orange. They are messing around. As I get close, the lights suddenly blink out.

"Hello? Are you the people from the jeep?"

No one answers me. I hear laughing in the far distance and look up to the hills. I see the shape of the jeep driving along with its four passengers.

A triangle of orange lights suddenly appears three metres in front of me. I stand very still. This is not the teenagers.

Each light flickers like a fire. Behind them, I can see something metal. Something big. I get a creepy feeling down my back. It's like I'm being watched. Like strange eyes are studying me.

Something rustles in the undergrowth nearby. My heart jumps. It's not a fox or an animal, it's moving on two feet. But not feet like mine. Twigs snap under its footsteps. It's going towards the lights.

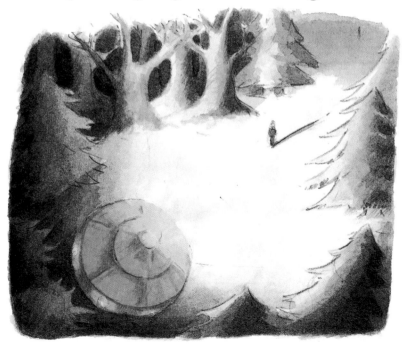

It races through the last of the
undergrowth and into the lights. They get
brighter. For just a second, I see its
silhouette.

I turn and run. I get ten metres when
my feet slip on the wet grass. I fall.

The ground is cold and hard. I have
frost on my hands. Above me, the
branches of the trees are silhouetted
against the sky. They look like alien
fingers reaching out to grab the stars.

Suddenly, there is a blast of noise like steam escaping. Then I feel a gust of really hot air. It keeps getting stronger.

I get up and run again. I look back, but I can't see anything because the wind hurts my eyes. They start to water.

I run uphill towards the thickest part of the woods. The last thing I remember is tripping on a tree root and the ground coming up towards me once more.

Epilogue – After

When I wake up, I really get it in the neck from Mum. The teenagers have found me and brought me back to the house.

I'm OK. Apart from the fact that one side of my face is kind of sun-burned. It doesn't hurt though.

Next morning, Mum drives us home. I sit in the back of the car and watch the clouds disappear over the horizon. I feel good.

Mum says that uncle's estate needs a lot of sorting out. She doesn't know that the most important thing has already been done.

Look out for more creepy titles in the Shivery Storybooks series:

Danny and the Sea of Darkness by David Clayton

One minute Danny's lying in bed, the next one he's thrashing about in a foaming sea. Why does he keep going back as Michael? And what will happen when he returns to the Sea of Darkness once more?

My Teacher the Ghost by Emma Fischel

Something strange is happening to Joey at Marvale School. Suddenly it's icy cold in the classroom and he has the creepy feeling he's being watched. Someone is haunting Joey, and they won't leave him alone...

The Ghost Bus by Anthony Masters

When Jack and Tina catch a late bus home from school, they very quickly realize that this is no ordinary bus. For a start, it's distinctly old fashioned, but worse, they can see right through their fellow passengers! They're on a ghost bus, a ghost bus with a mission...

The World's Smallest Werewolf by Stephen Bowkett

Tom and Ellie can't understand why everyone in Glenbarra seems so dark and secretive. But worse is to come when they find themselves surrounded by werewolves!

All these books and many more in the Storybooks series can be purchased from your local bookseller. For more information about Storybooks, write to: *The Sales Department, Macdonald Young Books, 61 Western Road, Hove, East Sussex BN3 1JD.*